© 2015 Chef Ricardo A. Adams

ISBN-13: 9780692431993
ISBN-10: 0692431993

Author
Chef Ricardo A. Adams

Editing & Design
Rainbow Creative Group

Photography
Chef Ricardo A. Adams

No part of this book may be reproduced in any form including, but not limited to, storage in a retrieval system in transmission, in any form or by any means, photocopied, mechanical, electronic, scanned, downloaded, recorded, or otherwise, without prior written permission from the publisher or authorization through payment of the appropriate per-copy fee to

Chef Ricardo Adams
6038 Cordova Road
Columbus, Georgia 31907
1-210-238-7912
Facebook Page: Chef Adams "Recipes For The Absolutely Terrified"
Twitter: Chef Ricardo A. Adams

Limit of Liability/Disclaimer of Warranty: While the author and publisher have used their best efforts in constructing this cookbook, they make no representations or warranties with respect to the accuracy or completeness of the contents of this book and specifically disclaim any implied warranties of merchantability or fitness for a particular purpose. No warranty may be created or extended by sales representatives or written sales materials. The advice and strategies contained herein may not be suitable for your situation. You should consult a professional where appropriate. Neither author nor publisher shall be liable for any loss or profit or any other commercial damages, including but not limited to special, incidental, consequential, or other damages.

To see Chef Adams cook his famous Crab Boil recipe as recorded on live TV

GO TO YouTube and view "The Dee Armstrong Show: Chef Ricardo Adams"

FOR MORE VIDEOS AND PICS, FOLLOW HIM ON FACEBOOK & TWITTER

Facebook: Chef Adams "Recipes For The Absolutely Terrified"
Twitter: Chef Ricardo A. Adams

ENJOY THE COOKBOOK

Contents

Fine Family Cuisine (p. 5)

The Menu (pp. 6-7)

Cooking Temperatures (p. 53)

Conversion Chart (p. 53)

Fine Family Cuisine

Barbecued pulled pork and slaw sandwiches, jambalaya, buffalo chicken wings, cheesecake, pecan pralines, even almond brittle to "Lobster Rockefeller!" All will make your taste buds go crazy, and that's just the beginning! These tried-and-true recipes will please everyone around the dinner table. While most recipes can be difficult and intimidating to attempt, in this cookbook Chef Ricardo A. Adams offers you a more subtle and down-to-earth approach to fine family cuisine. He encourages you to try and share these wonderful recipes—all compliments of the Adams family and their warm, loving hospitality.

The Menu

Apple-Stuffed Pork Loin with Cranberry Dressing 8

Tilapia and Veggies Wrapped in Banana Leaves 10

Barbecued Carolina Pulled Pork and Rickie's BBQ Sauce and Sandwich Slaw 12

Buffalo Chicken Wings 16

Braised Beef Ribs and Wet Sauce 18

Spicy Orange Carrot Sticks with Cilantro 20

Rickie's Scrumptious Potato Salad 21

Creole-Fashioned Jambalaya 22

Spaghetti with Seafood Marinara Sauce 24

Rickie's Famous Flounder Fillets 26

Rickie's Rockin' Sockin' Tarter Sauce 28

Lobster Rockefeller 29

Cucumber, Egg & Bacon Quick Salad 30

Crab Boil 32

Ultimate "Scraper" Patty Melt 33

The Menu

Rickie's Sassy Slaw 34

Orange Marmalade Chicken 35

Rickie's Cornbread Muffins 36

Italian Wedding Soup 38

Caldo de Res 40

Tortilla Soup 42

Shrimp 'n' Grits 44

Steamed Mussels 46

Almond Brittle 48

Rickie's New York-Style Cheesecake 50

Pecan Pralines 52

Apple-Stuffed Pork Loin with Cranberry Dressing

10 servings

INGREDIENTS

- 4 tbsp. of olive oil
- 1½ large red onion, diced
- 3 Granny Smith apples; peeled, cored and diced
- 10 fresh purple sage leaves
- 4 cups white bread, de-crusted and cubed
- 2 eggs, beaten well
- 2 tbsp. butter
- salt and pepper to taste (Gourmet Pepper Flake)
- 1 to 1½ cups chicken base, as needed
- 3 lb. pork loin roast, butterflied
- 1 cup dried cranberries
- bacon (optional to wrap around pork loin)*

DIRECTIONS

First preheat your oven to 375° F. Next, in a large skillet, heat up the olive oil over medium-high heat. Then add the onion, diced apples, and fresh sage leaves. Sauté until the fruit is transparent. Remove the skillet and moderately blend in the butter, bread, eggs, cranberries, salt, and pepper. Next, add the chicken stock slowly until everything is incorporated and moistened.

Let the stuffing cool completely.

Next, spoon the stuffing horizontally down the butterflied pork loin. Afterwards, roll the pork loin over the stuffing in a jelly roll fashion, resulting with the fat side up and with the pork seam down. Next, score the fat in diamond patterns. Firmly tie the pork loin with butcher's twine. Correct seasonings with salt and pepper.

Then transfer the pork onto a roasting pan. Roast the pork loin in the oven at 375° F for about 95 minutes or until an instant-read thermometer reads 165° F.

Remove the pork loin from the oven and let it rest for 15 minutes before serving.

Tilapia and Veggies Wrapped in Banana Leaves

8 servings

INGREDIENTS

- margarine, as needed
- 6 oz. red bell pepper, julienned
- 6 oz. leeks, julienned
- 6 oz. celery, julienned
- 8 oz. fennel bulb, julienned
- 6 oz. carrots, julienned
- 8 tilapia
- salt and pepper to taste
- basil butter with garlic
- lemon juice, as needed
- banana leaves

DIRECTIONS

First, wash all vegetables and deseed your bell pepper. Next, prepare eight banana leaves to envelop tilapia and veggies.

Then toss the julienned vegetables and place equal portions on half of each banana leaf. Place tilapia fillets over vegetables, then season with salt and pepper. Then top the tilapia with a tablespoon of basil and garlic butter. Dash with lemon juice.

Fold each banana leaf over and seal tightly with toothpicks. Place stuffed banana leaves on a sheet pan, then bake in a preheated oven at 450° F for 8 to 10 minutes.

Remove from oven, unwrap, and serve immediately.

Barbecued Carolina Pulled Pork and Rickie's BBQ Sauce and Sandwich Slaw

6 servings

INGREDIENTS FOR PULLED PORK

Dry Rub

- 2 tbsp. ground, course black pepper
- 2 tbsp. paprika
- 2 tbsp. dark brown sugar
- 3 tbsp. Kosher salt
- 1 tsp. cayenne pepper
- 3 lb. Boston butt
- seasoned salt
- vinegar
- red pepper

For the Mop

- ½ cup beer
- ¾ cup apple cider vinegar
- 1 tbsp. vegetable oil

- 2 tbsp. Worcestershire sauce
- 1 tbsp. black pepper
- 1 tsp. course salt
- 2 cups Rickie's BBQ Sauce (SEE PAGE 14)

Extras

- 6 hamburger buns, grilled

DIRECTIONS FOR PULLED PORK SANDWICH

First, mix dry ingredients to make a rub. Then sprinkle the rub over the pork while patting the seasonings into the meat. Wrap the meat in plastic wrap and let it marinate for 1 hour at room temperature. Next, mix the mop ingredients and set aside. Hot-smoke the pork with mesquite wood on the grill until fork-tender while brushing with the cold mop every 30 minutes. (Alternatively, you can bake your roast at 325° F for 3 hours or until fork-tender, brushing with cold mop every 30 minutes.)

Next, remove the meat from the grill or stove, and let it rest for 25 minutes. Finally, pull the meat apart with two forks or shred with a chef's knife. Next, combine the meat with Rickie's BBQ Sauce while covered; simmer 25 to 35 minutes. Add water as needed.

Serve pork on grilled buns with coleslaw and Rickie's BBQ Sauce.

Continued on next page...

INGREDIENTS FOR RICKIE'S BBQ SAUCE

- 1 tbsp. dry mustard
- 1 tbsp. course salt
- 2 cloves of garlic, crushed
- 4 sprigs of thyme
- 1½ tbsp. smoked paprika
- 1½ tbsp. sugar
- 1½ tbsp. brown sugar
- 1 tbsp. cayenne pepper
- 1 tsp. hot sauce (or as needed)
- ¾ cup molasses
- 2/3 cup red wine
- ½ cup Worcestershire sauce
- ¾ cup water
- 2 cups of catsup

DIRECTIONS

Mix the dry ingredients well in a saucepan. Gently stir in water; heat to boiling then remove from flame. Add wet ingredients.

INGREDIENTS FOR SANDWICH SLAW

- 3 cups green cabbage, shredded
- 3 tsp. sugar
- 3 tbsp. onions, diced
- 2 garlic cloves, minced
- 2 tsp. black pepper
- salt to taste
- 3 tbsp. cider vinegar
- 3 tbsp. mayonnaise
- 3 parsley sprigs, chopped
- 1 cup dried cranberries

DIRECTIONS

Mix all the ingredients then refrigerate for 45 minutes. Serve on the sandwiches or as a side dish.

Buffalo Chicken Wings

8 servings

INGREDIENTS

- 20 chicken wings
- 6 cups vegetable oil
- ½ cup margarine
- 4 tbsp. hot sauce
- ¾ cup syrup
- pinch of cayenne pepper to taste
- salt to taste (optional)

DIRECTIONS

Remove all chicken wing tips and reserve for chicken stock or for later use. Halve chicken wings. Heat oil approximately 375° F to 380° F and dry wings by patting with a paper towel. Fry until cooked golden crisp for 10 minutes. Drain oil from wings. If using liquid margarine, combine margarine, hot sauce, cayenne pepper, syrup, and vinegar in a bowl. If using stick margarine, melt the margarine over medium heat before combining the rest of the ingredients in a boiler. Toss chicken wings in the mixture and serve hot.

Braised Beef Ribs and Wet Sauce

4 slabs

INGREDIENTS

- 4 slabs beef ribs
- ½ cup vegetable oil
- flour for dusting
- seasoning salt and pepper to taste
- ¾ cup Jack Daniel's whiskey
- 2 cups onions, diced
- 1 cup carrots, diced and peeled
- ½ cup celery, diced
- 2 tsp. garlic, minced
- 3 tsp. all-purpose flour
- ¾ cup blanched tomatoes, diced and seeded
- 2 cups dry red wine
- 3 cups chicken stock
- 1½ tbsp. thyme leaves, chopped
- 1½ rosemary leaves, chopped

- 3 bay leaves
- 2 tsp. tomato paste
- 1 tsp. Montreal Steak Seasoning

DIRECTIONS

Season ribs with Montreal Steak Seasoning. Dust with flour. Then heat oil over high heat. Then brown ribs and reserve on a platter.

Reduce heat and sauté onions and carrots with Jack Daniel's whiskey. Then add celery and garlic. Sauté for 10 minutes. Flame for 20 seconds. Stir in flour and cook for 60 seconds. Add tomatoes, wine, thyme, rosemary, stock, bay leaves, tomato paste, seasoning salt, and pepper.

Bake or grill ribs until done. Then add the wet sauce.

Spicy Orange Carrot Sticks with Cilantro

6 servings

INGREDIENTS

- 1 cup orange juice
- 3 tbsp. sugar
- 2 tbsp. ginger, grated
- 5 cups carrots, julienned
- 3 tsp. cilantro, chopped
- salt and white pepper to taste
- pinch of cayenne pepper

DIRECTIONS

In a pot, combine carrots, ginger, cayenne pepper, orange juice, and sugar. Cover and cook until carrots are softened. Correct seasonings with salt and white pepper along with cilantro.

Rickie's Scrumptious Potato Salad

7 lbs.

INGREDIENTS

- 5 lbs. red-skinned potatoes
- 8 hard-boiled eggs
- 1 cup celery, diced
- 1 bunch green onions, sliced
- ½ cup granulated sugar (to taste)
- 2/3 cup course radishes, chopped
- 1 lb. mayonnaise
- ½ cup Dijon mustard
- ¼ cup fresh cilantro, chopped
- 3 Granny Smith apples
- paprika (optional)

Pototo salad served with Rickie's Famous Flounder Fillets and bread

DIRECTIONS

Wash potatoes then boil until slightly cooked. Drain the potatoes and refrigerate until cold. Dice potatoes. Combine all ingredients and adjust flavor. Top with sliced eggs. Lightly Sprinkle with paprika and cilantro (optional).

Creole-Fashioned Jambalaya

8 servings

INGREDIENTS

- 6 tbsp. vegetable oil
- 2 chicken fryers each cut into one-eighths
- 8 cups onions, diced
- 1 cup green peppers, diced
- 1/3 cup green onion, sliced
- 2 tbsp. garlic, minced
- 4 tbsp. cilantro, minced
- 1/3 cup baked ham, diced
- 2 ½ cups lean pork, cubed
- 6 cups smoked Polish sausage
- 1 bag of shrimp
- 4 tsp. salt
- 1 tsp. black pepper
- 1 tsp. cayenne pepper

- 1 tsp. chili powder
- 4 bay leaves
- 2 tsp. dried thyme
- ½ tbsp. ground cloves
- ½ tsp. dried basil
- ½ tbsp. mace
- 2 cups long-grain rice
- 6 cups chicken stock (preferably base)
- Old Bay Seasoning

DIRECTIONS

In a skillet, heat oil over medium heat. Then brown the chicken. Afterwards, remove. Add pork, ham, cilantro, shrimp, and vegetables. Stirring constantly, cook for 10 minutes over medium heat until everything is brown. For 5 minutes stirring constantly and scraping the bottom of the pan, add Old Bay Seasoning and sausage.

Next, add rice over medium heat. Cook for 7 minutes while constantly stirring and scraping the bottom of the pan. Add stock, chicken, the remainder of the herbs and spices, and bring to a boil. Cover the pot and turn down to simmer or bake at 350° F for 40 minutes while occasionally stirring.

Next, raise the heat to medium, uncover the pot, and cook 10 minutes, stirring very frequently. Remove bay leaves and serve hot.

Spaghetti with Seafood Marinara Sauce

5 servings

INGREDIENTS

- 9 oz. spaghetti
- 4 tbsp. olive oil
- 1½ onion, chopped
- 1 garlic clove, chopped
- 3½ cups tomato sauce
- 2 tbsp. tomato paste
- 1½ tsp. dried oregano
- 2 tbsp. Italian seasoning
- 2 tsp. sugar
- 3 cups shrimp, cooked and peeled
- 7 oz. cooked clam or mussels (or both)
- 2 tbsp. lemon juice
- 4 tbsp. parsley, chopped
- 3 tbsp. butter

- salt and black pepper to taste
- Old Bay Seasoning
- bay leaf
- 6 whole cooked shrimp to garnish
- a pinch of basil

DIRECTIONS

Heat olive oil in a saucepan, frying the onion and garlic for 8 minutes. In another saucepan, bring salted water to a boil and cook the spaghetti until tender. Stir Old Bay Seasoning, Italian seasoning, tomato paste, oregano, tomato sauce, bay leaf, and sugar into the onions, adding salt and pepper to taste. Bring to a boil, then simmer for 5 minutes.

As an alternative to seafood marinara sauce, you can use meatball sauce.

Add the shellfish, lemon juice, and 3 tbsp. of parsley. Cover and simmer for 8 minutes. Drain the spaghetti. Sauté the spaghetti and toss in butter. Plate up the spaghetti topped with sauce and garnish with shrimp, basil, and the remaining parsley.

Rickie's Famous Flounder Fillets

6 servings

INGREDIENTS

- 2 lbs. flounder fillets
- seasoning salt (as needed)
- 1 tsp. cayenne pepper
- flour (as needed)
- cornmeal (as needed)
- egg wash (as needed)
- 2 whole lemons

Chef's Tip: Same ingredients and directions can be used for shrimp.*

DIRECTIONS

First lay out three pans—one for the egg wash, one for the cornmeal, and the last for the flour. Season the fillets with seasoning salt. Add cayenne pepper to the cornmeal and mix well. Dip fillets into egg wash then into the cornmeal, then flour.

Deep-fry until done. Garnish with crowned lemons or sliced. Serve with hot sauce, ketchup and mustard, or tartar sauce.

Rickie's Rockin' Sockin' Tarter Sauce

1 pint

INGREDIENTS

- 1 pt. Hellman's Real Mayonnaise
- 3 oz. capers
- 4 oz. sweet pickle relish
- 3 tbsp. red onion, minced
- 3 tbsp. parsley, minced
- 1 tbsp. lemon juice
- sugar to taste
- Worcestershire sauce to taste
- Tabasco sauce to taste

DIRECTIONS

Stir all ingredients together and chill until serving.

Lobster Rockefeller

6 servings

INGREDIENTS

- 6 lobsters
- 4 cloves of garlic
- 4 tbsp. butter
- 6 sprigs chopped cilantro

DIRECTIONS

Mince garlic and add to butter, then reserve. Butterfly the lobster by cutting the shell using kitchen sheers, then slowly shuck lobster meat above shell carefully. Bake at 400° F about 8-10 minutes until done. Add garlic butter to lobster and sprinkle with chopped cilantro.

Cucumber, Egg & Bacon Quick Salad

5 servings

INGREDIENTS

- 1 tsp. black pepper
- pinch of salt to taste
- 1½ garlic cloves, minced
- 3½ tbsp. olive oil
- 1½ tbsp. red wine vinegar
- 1½ tbsp. lemon juice
- ½ cup green onions, diced
- 5 hard-boiled eggs, sliced
- 2/3 cup celery stalks with leaves, diced
- 7 red radishes, sliced
- 4 strips bacon, diced
- 1 head of Boston (Bibb) lettuce, shredded
- 3 tomatoes, sliced
- 1 cucumber, sliced

DIRECTIONS

Rinse all vegetables. Mix salt, pepper, vinegar, garlic, lemon juice, olive oil, and green onions. Combine the eggs, celery, radishes, cucumber, and lettuce with one-half of the dressing. Fan tomatoes on each plate top with egg/lettuce mixture garnished with bacon. Drizzle remaining dressing.

Crab Boil

6 servings

INGREDIENTS

- crab meat (legs, frozen, etc.) (as much as you want)
- 1 lb. corn on the cob, cut into thirds
- 1 lb. potatoes
- 10 oz. sausage of your choice
- 1 lb. shrimp, peeled and de-veined
- Old Bay Seasoning to taste
- 3 bay leaves
- Cajun seasoning to taste
- margarine, as needed
- chopped parsley, as needed

DIRECTIONS

First cook corn and potatoes until tender. Add as much crab as you want. After 5 minutes add sausage. After 5 minutes add shrimp. Add Old Bay Seasoning. Add bay leaves to boil with Cajun seasoning to taste. Afterwards, toss in margarine and chopped parsley.

Ultimate "Scraper" Patty Melt

1 serving

INGREDIENTS

- 2 BLTs (bacon, lettuce, tomato sandwiches) on Cheddar cheese-toast
- 2 buns
- mayo
- 2 pickles
- 2 grilled 100% Angus beef patties
- 2 slices Swiss cheese
- 2 slices bacon
- mushrooms
- two over-easy eggs
- salt and pepper
- brown gravy
- onion rings or fried green tomatoes

DIRECTIONS

Grill hamburger patties and bacon, sauté mushrooms, and then set everything aside. Bring to boil one package of brown gravy. Then grill toast, adding bacon, lettuce, and Cheddar cheese, to make BLT. Deep-fry onion rings or fried-green tomatoes, then fry eggs over-easy. Stack ingredients and dagger with steak knife, topping knife with onion rings or tomatoes.

Rickie's Sassy Slaw

3 lbs.

INGREDIENTS

- 1 cup mayonnaise
- ½ cup sour cream
- ½ cup sugar
- 2½ tbsp. apple cider vinegar
- 1 lb. green cabbage, shredded
- 1½ cup red cabbage, shredded
- 1 tsp. mild brown mustard
- ¾ cup carrots, shredded
- salt and pepper to taste
- 1 cup dried cranberries
- 1 garlic clove, minced

DIRECTIONS

Combine mayonnaise, mustard, sour cream, sugar, cranberries, vinegar, and garlic, then whisk together. Add shredded carrots and cabbages to the dressing. Adjust seasonings. Serve cold.

Orange Marmalade Chicken

1 chicken

INGREDIENTS

- 1 whole chicken
- 1 orange, sliced and grilled
- 1 cup orange marmalade
- 2 tbsp. margarine
- Worcestershire sauce to taste
- salt and pepper
- 1 tbsp. sugar
- parsley

DIRECTIONS

Mildly season the chicken with salt and pepper. Mix marmalade, margarine, Worcestershire sauce, and sugar together and toss the chicken in the mixture. Bake in the oven at 350° F for about an hour until chicken reaches 165° temp. Garnish with orange slices and parsley.

Rickie's Cornbread Muffins

 12 muffins

INGREDIENTS

- 1½ cups yellow cornmeal
- 1½ cups all-purpose flour
- 3½ tsp. double-acting baking powder
- ½ cup sugar
- 1 pinch salt
- 1¼ cup milk
- 1 large egg
- 1/3 cup vegetable oil
- 1/3 cup onions, shredded
- liquid or melted margarine to brush over muffins

DIRECTIONS

Grease and heat a 12-mold muffin tin. Mix together flour, sugar, baking powder, cornmeal, and salt in a bowl. In another bowl, whisk milk, egg, vegetable oil, and onions. Combine both mixtures. Distribute evenly in the muffin tin and bake for 25 minutes at 400° F. Brush muffins with margarine.

Italian Wedding Soup

3 servings

INGREDIENTS

Meatballs

- 2 lbs. ground beef
- 2 lbs. ground pork
- 1 cup dried breadcrumbs
- 2 tbsp. flat-leaf parsley, chopped
- 2 tbsp. Parmesan cheese, grated
- 2 tbsp. garlic, chopped
- 1½ tbsp. oregano, chopped
- ¼ tsp. salt
- ¼ tsp. pepper
- ¼ tsp. Italian seasoning
- ½ egg, beaten
- pinch of ground nutmeg
- pinch of paprika

Soup

- 1½ tbsp. margarine
- ½ cup white onions, chopped
- ½ cup carrots, chopped
- 1½ tbsp. garlic, chopped
- salt and pepper to taste
- 2 cups chicken stock
- 1 (14 oz.) can whole tomatoes, halved
- ½ cup uncooked orzo
- 1 cup kale, shredded

DIRECTIONS

In a large bowl, mix all meatball ingredients together. Measure the meatballs with a teaspoon. Pan up and refrigerate.

In a large soup pot on medium heat, melt the margarine for the soup. Add carrots, garlic, onions, salt and pepper, and simmer for 5 minutes. Add chicken stock, tomatoes, and 1 cup of water. Cook for 10 minutes until soup boils. Add orzo, meatballs to the soup. Cover for 20 minutes over medium heat. Add kale. Serve immediately.

Caldo de Res

6 servings

INGREDIENTS

- 2 piece beef shank or chuck
- 5 red-skinned potatoes
- 3 carrots, peeled
- 2 onions, peeled
- 3 qts. cold water
- 2 corn on the cob, cleaned
- 1 tbsp. thyme
- 2 bay leaves
- 2 parsley sprigs
- 2 cups green cabbage
- 1 cup zucchini, cubed
- salt and pepper to taste
- 2 tbsp. lime juice
- 3 tbsp. cilantro, chopped

DIRECTIONS

Wash and boil vegetables and meat. Place potatoes in a pot of cold water. Add salt and pepper, thyme, parsley, and bay leaves. Let simmer. After tender, remove ingredients from the pot.

Let vegetables cool, then dice. Dice meat then return veggies and meat back to the broth. Cook 1 hour 30 minutes. Let simmer. Add zucchini and remove the bay leaves. Before serving, add lime juice and cilantro.

Tortilla Soup

6 servings

INGREDIENTS

- 1¼ cups onion, quartered
- 2½ plum tomatoes, quartered
- ½ cup vegetable oil
- 2 corn tortillas cut into strips
- 3 garlic cloves, minced
- 1 ancho chili; stemmed, seeded, toasted, and chopped
- 1 bay leaf
- 1 tsp. ground cumin
- 4 cups of chicken stock
- ½ cup tomato sauce
- salt and pepper to taste
- 2½ cups cooked chicken meat, julienned
- 1½ cups Monterey Jack cheese, shredded

- 1½ cups avocado, peeled, pitted, cubed
- 1½ cups crisp tortilla chips for garnish

DIRECTIONS

First rinse tomatoes. Then rub tomatoes and onion with oil. Grill and char 15 to 20 minutes. Afterwards, blend in a blender and sit aside. Heat the vegetable oil, adding garlic, tortilla and chile 3 to 4 minutes to sauté. Add stock, cumin, bay leaf and bring to a boil. Stir in tomato sauce and mixture. Correct seasonings. Heat soup and serve. Garnish with chicken, avocado, cheese, and crisp tortilla chips.

Shrimp 'n' Grits

5 servings

INGREDIENTS

- 1 lb. shrimp, peeled and de-veined
- grits to serve
- 2 strips of bacon, chopped
- 2 patties of sausage, chopped
- 1 garlic clove, minced
- ½ onion, crushed
- 2 tsp. margarine, or as needed
- Old Bay Seasoning
- thyme to taste
- Cajun seasoning
- chicken base to taste
- cheddar cheese, to garnish
- parsley to garnish

DIRECTIONS

Boil grits in chicken base following cooking time instructions on your package. Cook sausage and bacon. Sauté shrimp. Sauté one-half onion and garlic. Add all of this to the grits along with margarine and add seasonings. Garnish with cheese and parsley.

Steamed Mussels

3 servings

INGREDIENTS

- 3 lbs. cleaned mussels
- 10 fl oz. dry white wine
- 2 oz. garlic, chopped
- 1 tsp. white pepper
- 6 sprigs fresh thyme
- 3 bay leaves
- 5 oz. margarine
- 2 tbsp. parsley, chopped
- 2 oz. coconut milk
- 1 tsp. Old Bay Seasoning
- 3 leaks, steamed and julienned
- 1 carrot, steamed and julienned

DIRECTIONS

Combine all ingredients and bring to a boil, stirring the mussels until they open. Arrange the mussels into soup bowls, leaving the leaks and carrots to garnish on top. Sprinkle with parsley.

Almond Brittle

2½ lbs.

INGREDIENTS

- 2½ cups granulated sugar
- 1 cup light corn syrup
- 1 cup water
- 1½ cups almonds
- 1 tsp. salt
- 1 tsp. baking soda
- 1 tbsp. margarine
- 1 tsp. baking powder
- 1 tsp. baking soda
- 2 tsp. vanilla extract

DIRECTIONS

Combine corn syrup, sugar, and water. Cook to dissolve sugar over medium heat. Cook to the soft ball stage (238° F, 114° C). Add almonds and salt. Stirring constantly, cook until the hard crack stage (300° F, 419° C).

Remove from heat and stir in margarine, baking soda, baking powder, and vanilla. Pour onto wax paper or silpat. Once hardened, break into pieces! Enjoy!

Rickie's New York-Style Cheesecake

1 cake

INGREDIENTS FOR CRUST

- 7 oz. Graham Cracker crumbs
- 3 oz. melted margarine

DIRECTIONS FOR CRUST

Combine melted margarine and Graham Cracker crumbs. Press evenly over the bottom and sides of the pan.

INGREDIENTS FOR CHEESECAKE

- 2 lbs. cream cheese, room temp
- 1 lb. sugar
- 1 oz. cornstarch
- lemon zest
- 3 tsp. vanilla extract
- 2 eggs, room temp

- 4 egg yolks, room temp
- 3½ oz. sour cream
- fruit or blueberry sauce

DIRECTIONS FOR CHEESECAKE

On low speed, mix the cream cheese and sugar using a paddle until smooth. Mix in cornstarch, lemon zest, and vanilla extract until smooth. Add eggs and egg yolks. Add sour cream. Pan up the batter. Inside hotel pans, add pan while administering hot water one-half way up the side of the pans. Bake at 300° F for 1-1/2 hours. Cool, chill, and remove the cake from the pan. Decorate with fruit, blueberry/strawberry sauce, or chocolate mint.

Pecan Pralines

6 servings

INGREDIENTS

- 1½ cup brown sugar
- 1 cup granulated sugar
- ¼ tsp. salt
- ¾ cup heavy cream
- ¼ tsp. cream of tartar
- 1½ cup of pecan pieces
- 3 tbsp. butter
- 1 tbsp. vanilla extract

DIRECTIONS

In a heavy pan, combine cream of tartar, salt, sugars, and cream. Stir over low heat with a rubber spatula. Cook until the soft ball stage (234° F, 240° C) over medium heat. Add pecans and cook for 3 minutes. Remove from heat. Add butter and vanilla extract. Beat until mixture becomes creamy. Drop the candy onto wax paper. Once cool, cut the paper, wrap, and serve.

Cooking Temperatures

Chicken	165° F	74° C
Beef, veal, lamb, roast, lamb	145° F	63° C
Pork, ham, bacon	145° F*	63° C*
Smoked ham, beef rare	145° F	60° C
Fish	145° F*	63° C*

*For 15 seconds

Metric Conversion Chart

Volume Measurements (Dry)

1/8 tsp. = 0.5 mL
¼ tsp. = 1 mL
½ tsp. = 2 mL
¾ tsp. = 4 mL
1 tsp. = 5 mL
1 tbsp. = 15 mL
2 tbsp. = 30 mL
¼ cup = 60 mL
1/3 cup = 75 mL
½ cup = 125 mL
2/3 cup = 150 mL
¾ cup = 175 mL
1 cup = 250 mL
2 cups = 1 pt = 500 mL
3 cups = 750 mL
4 cups = 1 quart

Volume Measurements (Fluid)

1 fluid ounce (2 tbsp.) = 30 mL
4 fluid ounces (½ cup) = 125 mL
8 fluid ounces (1 cup) = 250 mL
12 fluid ounces (1½ cups) = 375 mL
16 fluid ounces (2 cups) = 500 mL

For more great recipes & pics go to Facebook & Twitter

Facebook Page:
Chef Adams "Recipes For The Absolutely Terrified"

Twitter:
Chef Ricardo A. Adams

Made in the USA
Las Vegas, NV
23 December 2023